YOUR KNOWLEDGE HAS VALUE

AF144758

- We will publish your bachelor's and master's thesis, essays and papers

- Your own eBook and book - sold worldwide in all relevant shops

- Earn money with each sale

Upload your text at www.GRIN.com and publish for free

Bibliographic information published by the German National Library:

The German National Library lists this publication in the National Bibliography; detailed bibliographic data are available on the Internet at http://dnb.dnb.de .

Imprint:

Copyright © 2016 GRIN Verlag, Open Publishing GmbH
Print and binding: Books on Demand GmbH, Norderstedt Germany
ISBN: 978-3-668-19913-2

This book at GRIN:

http://www.grin.com/en/e-book/320642/landeskundliche-themen-fuer-das-abitur-im-fach-englisch-eine-lernzusammenfassung

Anonym

Landeskundliche Themen für das Abitur im Fach Englisch. Eine Lernzusammenfassung in Stichpunkten

GRIN Publishing

GRIN - Your knowledge has value

Since its foundation in 1998, GRIN has specialized in publishing academic texts by students, college teachers and other academics as e-book and printed book. The website www.grin.com is an ideal platform for presenting term papers, final papers, scientific essays, dissertations and specialist books.

Visit us on the internet:

http://www.grin.com/

http://www.facebook.com/grincom

http://www.twitter.com/grin_com

ENGLISCH THEMENÜBERSICHT

Abitur GK & LK

Inhaltsverzeichnis

1. American Traditions and Visions – The American Dream

1.1. The American Dream

1.1.1. Definition

- In 1931 first used by James Truslow Adams (In his Book: *"The Epic of America"*)
    - "The American Dream is the dream of a land in which life should be better and richer and fuller for every man with opportunity for each according to his ability or achievement."
- no single definition – varies for every Individual
- Core element is that if a person works hard enough he/she will achieve his/her goals and improve his/her position in life

1.1.2. Quotations

- "From a dishwasher to a millionaire."
- "From rags to riches."
- "All men are created equal."

1.2. The American Dream Then and Now

1.2.1. Then

- The early settlers in America hoped for a better life than the one they had left behind in Europe. They dreamt about:
    - The personal dream of freedom, self-fulfillment, dignity and happiness
    - The economic dream of prosperity and success ("from rags to riches")
    - The religious dream of religious freedom in a "promised land" in which they were God's chosen people
    - The social dream of equality and a classless society
    - The political dream of democracy

1.2.2. Now

- The American Dream has come to be seen more critically
    - Critics regard: American Dream is an illusion
- Multiculturalism: relates to communities containing multiple cultures
- Multicultural society: society where multiculturalism is accepted
- Salad bowl: integration of many different cultures of the US residents combine like a salad
- Melting pot: various ethnic groups amalgamate into one new nation
- Assimilation: language and culture of a person come to resemble those of another
- E pluribus unum: "out of many, one"

1.3. American Nightmare Visions

- Bad health care system
- Terror
- Economic problems
    - Bank crisis/ debts
    - Gap between poor and rich
    - Financial crises (i.e. 2008)
- Big gap between dream and reality
- Racism/no equality
    - Black and white
    - Slavery

     o   Immigration

     ⇨ No American Dream for Mexicans and African Americans

1.4. Does the American Dream come true – NOW?

- No classless society ⇨ lower classes are the losers in the race of success
- Huge diversity in income and lifestyle
- Hard work for middle class to live the American way
- Vision of America as a "melting pot"(immigrants give up their identity) didn't become reality
  → Immigrants get more self-confident
  → New concept: "Salad bowl" (multicultural America)
- critics see the American Dream as a clever political and marketing strategy
- want people to get away from selfish individualism and materialism
- huge gap between rich and poor is obvious, but the role of state welfare and political intervention in helping weaker members of society remains controversial – society is marked by the ambition to succeed
- more and more illegal immigrations – used as a cheap workers
- real American Dream of giving up national identity, way of life or culture and language has never become reality
  ⇨ The American Dream is for some people only an illusion

1.5. Historical landmarks of the American Dream

1776	Foundation of the declaration of Independence
1789	Constitution establishes the principles of a democratic government
1791	Foundation of the Bill of Rights
1790 – 1890	After Revolutionary War (1776-1783) Americans start to move westward and to settle the vast North American continent (⇨ "the Frontier")
1865	Slavery is legally abolished (at the end of the Civil War)
1869	Right of full voting are given to women in Wyoming
1870	Voting Rights were extended to all adult males of all races
1933	Roosevelt aims to overcome the extreme poverty and inequalities that resulted from the Great Depression of the 1920s
1964	Racial segregation are banned´; legal discrimination is abolished
1960s/1970s	Younger generation of Americans increasingly reject the traditional values of their parents and the government

1.6. Important Documents

1.6.1. Bill of Rights

- First ten amendments to the American Constitution (Amendments known as the Bill of Right)
- Written because some delegates feared restriction of personal freedom and the pursuit of happiness
- Guarantee America's citizens certain unalienable rights, e.g. freedom of religion, speech and press and right to bear arms

1.6.2. Declaration of Independence

- Written in 1776 by Thomas Jefferson
- All American citizens are created equal (personal rights)
- Possibility for every American to lead his life the way he wants to, by making his own personal dreams come true

- 1776: 13 colonies declared their independence from England and were at war with England
- Questioned the rights of the British monarch (revolutionary at the time)

1.7. Incidental Matters

1.7.1. Manifest Destiny

- Belief that America is the one nation ordered by God to expand across the North American continent
- America = a country that is superior to all other countries
- Stresses virtue of the American people, as they are the ones to establish moral rules and values across the globe
- American patriotism is deeply rooted in the concept of "Manifest Destiny"

1.7.2. The Frontier

- Pacific coast was reached in the 2nd half of the 19th century
- After this mission
  → New challenges – new frontiers – were needed (e.g. space exploration (moon landing), scientific and technological progress)

1.7.3. The Puritans

- Puritan's beliefs and values had a lasting impact on New England society
- Towards the end of 16th century some English Protestants felt that Protestantism in England was not much different from Catholicism
  ⇨ Decided to leave England, seeking their luck elsewhere
- Wished to remain English subjects but free to worship God the way they wanted to
  ⇨ Intention: to purify the Church of England, not to leave it
- September 1620: group of 102 people left England for America (sailed on a ship Mayflower), arrived in America 65 days later, in a bay called Plymouth Bay

1.7.4. The New Canaan

- Canaan was the Land God promised to the Israelites, the place where Moses led his people when God told him to free them from the Egyptian slavery
- A land of milk and honey
- People who flew of religious persecution to America called it "New Canaan" – hope that America will become "promised land"
- Closely linked to the idea of "manifest destiny"

1.7.5. Statue of Liberty

- First thing many immigrants saw when they came by ship to New York City during the 19th and the first half of the 20th century, was the Statue of Liberty (located on Liberty Island)
- A robed woman, holding a lit torch in her right and a tablet in her left hand -> showing the date of the Declaration of Independence (July 4, 1776)
- One of the most famous American icons, symbolizing enlightenment, independence, liberty and freedom

6

1.7.6. Ellis Island

- the place where most immigrants first set foot on American soil
- an island of hopes but also an island of tears for a number of immigrants
- some of them were detained there for legal, or medical reasons or sent back
- the gateway to a new – better – life for the majority of the immigrants

2. British Traditions and Visions

2.1. History

15th century	First maritime explorations of the British Empire
1607	First permanent settlement of the British Empire in the USA => **"First British Empire"**
17th century	British Empire founded colonies in Northern America and in the Caribbean, which were controlled by the English crown and should bring ray materials to Britain
1781	End of the **"First British Empire"** with the **Declaration of Independence** of the Northern American colonies

18th and 19th century	British colonialism had expanded around the whole globe, with different types of colonies which were under the direct rule of Britain (New Imperialism and **"Second British Empire"**) :
	 - Settlement colonies
	   o E.g. Canada, Australia, New Zeeland
	 - Trading colonies
	   o E.g. India: Spices, cotton, tea
	 - Strategically important colonies
	   o E.g. Gibraltar, Malta, Cyprus, the Suez Canal

⇨ **The British Empire** was the largest Empire in History ⇨ Division of the whole world: competition in building new colonies	
1947 (After World War II)	End of the second British Empire with the **Independence of India**
⇨ Commonwealth come off the Empire	

2.2. From Empire to Commonwealth

2.2.1. Empire

- Britain ⇨Powerful; Wealthy; Defeated other nations ⇨ gained supremacy; Industrial Revolution ⇨ Technological advances

2.2.2. Dissolution of Empire

- After World War II ⇨ Colonies were eager for independence and freedom
- British thought: Colonies are developed enough to govern themselves on their own
- High war costs prevented a British reign of the whole world

2.2.3. The Commonwealth

- Follower of the British empire (founded in 1931)
- Group of 53 independent states ⇨ many former British colonies joined at the end
- The British Queen is the head of the commonwealth
- Reasons for joining:
  - Commercial reasons; protection; no economic or political advantages
- Aims:
  - Racial equality; national sovereignty

2.3. The political system in Great Britain

2.3.1. The monarchy

2.3.1.1. The monarchy

- Oldest institution of the government in Britain in which the supreme power or sovereignty is held by a single person.

2.3.1.2. The monarch

- The monarch has no overt power but is formally part of the government system.
- The monarch is the:
  o Head of State
  o Symbol of national unity
  o Head of the executive and judiciary
  o Commander-in-chief of the armed forces
  o "supreme governor" of the Church of England

2.3.1.3. Duties of the monarch

- He/she appoints the prime minister
- He/she summons and dissolves Parliament
- He/she gives Royal Assent tot legislation
- He/she formally appoints ministers, judges, officers, diplomats, bishops
- etc.

2.3.1.4. Advantages and disadvantages of a monarchy

Advantages	Disadvantages
Stability, continuity	Lack of democratic accountability
Impartiality	A job for life
Minimal (=less) chances for corruption	The living of the royal family is very expensive
Queen is an idol	Old-fashioned class system
Tourist attraction	Not important for governmental decisions

2.3.2. Main political Parties

2.3.2.1. Tories ⇨ the Conservative Party

  o Right-wing Party
  o Associated with:
    ▪ Nationalism
    ▪ Law and order
    ▪ Private enterprise
    ▪ Minimal interference of the state in the economy

2.3.2.2. Whigs ⇨ the Labour Party

  o Traditional party of the "working class"
  o Associated with:
    ▪ State control and planning
    ▪ Nationalization of key industries
    ▪ Welfare
    ▪ Affiliation of the trade unions

2.3.3. The Parliament

2.3.3.1. House of Lords

- Upper chamber of Parliament
- Made up of 1171 non-elected-peers
- Function: make amendments to a bill and return it to House of Commons
- Final court of appeal for civil cases
- Debates on matters of politics

Advantages	Disadvantages
"moderator" against rash legislation	Does not represent the electorate
Revising chamber	Preserves class distinction
Inflicting defeats on government	Members can't take part at the elections
Opinions can be expressed more freely than in House of Commons	

2.3.3.2. House of Commons

- Consists of 650 members of Parliament (MPs) which are elected by people

2.4. Britain and the EU

2.4.1. Facts

- Traditionally Britain had preferred to stay out of the EU
- Economic reasons has been forced Britain into the EU in 1973
- Britain has joined the monetary union (i.e. they don't have the Euro as currency)
- Britain has not signed the Schengen Agreement, which permits travelling without border control between 25 European countries
- Many of the British don't want to be a member of the EU
- Britain is not interested in helping EU

2.4.2. Arguments of the Eurosceptics and in favour of the European Union

A. Of the Eurosceptics	A. in favour of the European Union
The EU is expensive to run	The End of war between European nations
The EU is dominated by big countries at the expense of smaller members	Democracy is now flourishing in 27 countries
The EU is too powerful	The creation of the world's largest internal trading market
The EU is trying to impose regulation in policy areas that should be the responsibility of national governments (e.g. health, education, law, tax)	Co-operation on continent-wide immigrations policy
The EU is corrupt and money-wasting	Co-operation on crime, through Europol
The EU is a security risk with its open borders	Laws that make it easier for British people to buy property in Europe
The EU is host to millions of immigrants, some of them hostile and violent	Cleaner beaches and river throughout Europe
The EU is undemocratic	Unparalleled rights for European consumers

3. Post-colonialism and Migration

3.1. India important facts

- Unique country that is easily accessible to other parts of Asia, Africa, Europe and America
- Official languages are Hindi and English, a few of the others are Marathi, Bengali, Urdu etc.
- Four main religions are Hinduism, Islam, Christianity and Sikhism
- Currency is the Indian rupee (INR)

3.2. India's present situation

Good	Bad
Many millionaires in cities	High corruption and crime rate
Nuclear and economic superpower	overpopulation
Growing middle class	Environmental problems
English language is one of the official languages	Not high developed country (developing country)
Many jobs are outsourced to India	Exploitation and illiteracy
World's most advanced technology (with IT specialists and well-trained engineers	Arranged marriages and discrimination against women
	Cheap/child labour
	Extreme social disparities between rich and poor people (in slums for example)

3.3. Indian history

3.3.1. British Empire

- Founding of colonies for military reasons
- America wanted to be independent
- Separation of the American colonies from the British
- Other colonies wanted to be independent too
- End of Empire: Independence of India

3.3.2. Partition (India and Pakistan)

- India and Pakistan were founded in 1947
- Partition led to riots and mass migration to India (Hindu) or Pakistan (Muslim)depending on religion because the people feared religious persecution
- India and Pakistan quarrelled over Jammu and Kashmir because the maharajah still had not decided which state to join. After the maharajah had joined India, Indian-Pakistan war came into existence
- Division accompanied by emigration and massacres
- Supporters of India's independence (Ghandi and Nehru) were not able to avoid the division of the Indian subcontinent

3.4. Migration

3.4.1. Immigration to England

- Immigration wave started in the 1950s; peak at the beginning of the 1960s
- Largest group are Indians ⇨ first wave started shortly after having gained independence
- Third largest group are Pakistanis and Bangladeshis
- High increase in population led to intensification of immigration rules

- Many Pakistani live in the West Midlands and in Greater London
  ⇨ "Asian suburbs" didn't afford integration

3.4.2. Reasons for immigration

- Division of India and foundation of Pakistan in 1947
- Building of the Mangla barrage ⇨ displacement of people
- Persecution in India
- to re-join members of their family, who already live there
- to learn something about other cultures
- to get a better living standard (better education, better wages etc.)

3.4.3. Migration today

- Britain represents the strongest colonial power in the history
- British culture, politics and social structures were adapted in the colonies and survived in the former colonies
- Many migrants choose Britain as destination
- New anti-discrimination legislation was introduced

3.5. Caste System

- Indian society is divided into different groups (called Jatis)
- Separation of society in education, marriage, health care, life expectancy and more
- Industrial revolution and economic boom weaken the caste system
- All castes had to avoid any contact with the "untouchables" and vice versa

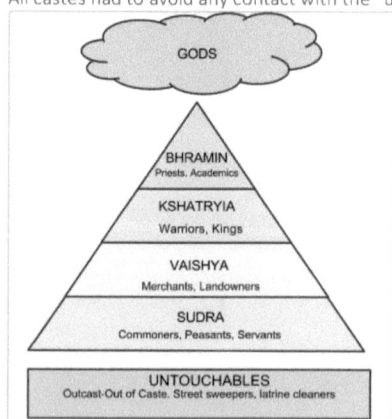

3.6. Arranged marriage

- Part of tradition
- Often by high-caste people in order to protect their status
- In older times, parents decided without consent
- Nowadays, children are asked for their consent

Pros	Cons
Economic aspect	Don't know each other very well
Family status stays in social class	No change of the system ⇨ no mixed status
Easier to marry ⇨ more children	No chance for "real love"

11

Good cooperation with parents-in-law	Kids are long dependent⇨parents take control
Love grows after marriage	Whole family is involved

4. Globalization – Global Challenges

4.1. Definition

- Globalization represents the largest economic and social shift since the Industrial Revolution. It is a process of growing links between societies and problem areas and a process of surmounting limitations created by history. Furthermore it is a process by which the world is becoming increasingly interconnected as a result of massively increased trade and cultural change and is often seen as an unstoppable process which is affecting people all around the globe (industrialized as well as developing countries)."

4.2. Keywords

- Sweat-shop:
  o Workplace with poor working conditions. The work may be difficult, dangerous or underpaid. Workers in sweatshops may work long hours with low pay or a minimum wage.
- Developing country
- Industrial country
- Outsourcing:
  o Delivery of enterprise duties and enterprises structures to external or internal service providers (also third-party-companies)
- Global player:
  o Corporations, which are represented in the whole world and are not only firms, but have subsidiaries in many countries (McDonalds, H&M, etc.)
- Global village:
  o World as a single community in which people are connected by modern telecommunication (television, internet, etc.)
- Ecological footprint:
  o Measures the total amount of land in relation to the lifestyle of the people, in order to calculate what portion of the planet's resources we consume
- Climate change:
  o Climate change means changes in temperature, extreme weather events, which has effects on glaciers, the sea levels, flooding, forest fires etc.

4.3. Types of globalization

- Economic globalization:
  o activity of the multinational companies (=global players)
  o constant pressure to cut costs ⇨ priorities: efficiency, speed, flexibility, profits
  o employees' welfare and job security not important

- Technological globalization:
  o rapid advances in technology
  o microelectronics revolution ⇨ more easy and efficient communication by computer or mobile phone

- Cultural globalization:
  o spread of previously local or national cultural phenomena around the world (sports, art, fashion, religion, music)

4.4. Economic and cultural Issues

- **Economic issues:**
  - o The free trade comes at the expense of workers in developing countries ⇨ long working hours, unsafe and unhealthy working conditions in sweatshops, low wages
  - o Child labour in developing countries
  - o Mass production entails outsourcing of factories (production in developing countries)
  - o competition between companies (entails low prices for consumers)
  - o Rapid development of technological innovations ⇨ microelectronics allow consumers and people to communicate, to exchange information or to distribute information more easily (Internet, mobile phone, computer etc.)

- **Ecological issues:**
  - o Environmental pollution is growing rapidly due to globalization...
    - ▪ Exhaust fumes because of the increasing number of vehicles
  - o Global warming
  - o Threatened biodiversity
  - o Lack of diminishing resources
  - o Sustainable environmental influence....
    - ▪ Due to ... areas deteriorate and become useless (=desertification):
      - • Overgrazing, Over-extraction of groundwater, waste of resources; Deforestation ("slash-and-burn-farming") ; Rising soil salinity ; Use of Nuclear Energy

4.5. Eras of globalization

- 1st globalization (1492-1800)
  - o countries competing with each other / struggle for colonies
  - o global competition
  - o a countries brawn ; strength

- 2nd globalization (1800-2000)
  - o multinational companies struggle for profit
  - o industrialization
  - o expansion
  - o first: global economy, steam engine, railroads
  - o then: communication, transport costs

- 3rd globalization (since 2000)
  - o global competition among individuals
  - o individuals try to find their place in a globalized world
  - o more opportunities to work

4.6. Trigger and Promoter of the globalization

- improvement in transportation
- freedom of trade
- improvement of communication

4.7. Pros and Cons of globalization

- **Pros:**
  - o **Economy:** new jobs and skills; economic growth ⇨ improving living standards in developing countries; expansion of trade; global financial markets; allows to increase economies; transnational transaction; free trade; access to products from different countries; growing prosperity for producers
  - o **Politics:** less conflicts between nations ⇔ global agendas
  - o **Technology:** technological development; faster exchange of information ⇨ time and space are no longer a barrier ⇨ business and transaction easier; technical progress (innovations) ⇨ more machines; transport becomes easier and quicker
  - o **Culture:** people have become more tolerant against other cultures, religions, etc.; sharing of ideas, experiences, lifestyles of people and cultures

- **Cons:**
  - o **Economy:** only minority benefits from the globalization process ⇨ 'survival of the fittest'; financial crises could affect the whole world negatively; environmental problems ⇨ negative impact on environment and economy; people in industrial countries lose jobs; unfair working conditions; dependency on other countries
  - o **Politics:** welfare state is on retreat; no international laws
  - o **Technology:** changes are too fast ⇨ stress of workers; fewer people are needed in the production ⇨ people become unemployed or have to work harder for low wages in worse conditions; more transport ⇨ higher emissions
  - o **Culture:** clash of cultures ⇨ misunderstanding ; racism, xenophobia (Ausländerfeindlichkeit); human rights and safety standards are ignored, unfair working conditions; loss of identity; gap between poor and rich ⇨ rich are getting richer and poor are getting poorer ⇨ middle-classes disappear; fear of losing culture and traditions; fear of illegal immigrants come into industrial countries

4.8. Global warming and its consequences

4.8.1.Global warming

- Greenhouse gases form a layer around the earth trapping heat & thereby causing the temperature on the earth to rise

4.8.2. Consequences of global warming:

- Extreme weather conditions; Hurricanes & storms get stronger and more frequent
- Rising of sea level: Floods, heavy rainfall, drought, (wild)fires, melting of polar icecaps
- Biodiversity is threatened, many animals & plants become endangered or extinct
- Increase of diseases

4.9. How to slow the climate change ⇨ measures

Don'ts :	Do's:
- drive alone in your car	- car sharing
- drive a car	- ride a bike, walk
- buy food from far away	- buy local food
- take a bath	- take a shower
- use a plastic bag	- use a cloth bag/recycled bag
- let the TV on when you go away	- turn the TV off when you go away
- put bananas, apples etc. in the bin	- put bananas, apples, etc. in the compost

- put sth. in the bin	- recycle

4.10.   Some alternative/renewable energies

- **Wind Power**
  - o Wind energy harnesses the power of the wind to propel the blades of wind turbines. The rotation of turbine blades power electric generators.
- **Solar Power**
  - o It works by trapping the sun's rays into solar cells where this sunlight is then converted into electricity.
- **Geothermal power**
  - o Hot rocks under the ground heat water to produce steam. When holes are drilled in the region, the steam that shoots up is purified and is used to drive turbines, which power electric generators.
- **Hydroelectric power**
  - o Hydro power works by harnessing the gravitational descent of a river that is compressed from along run to a single location with a dam or a flume. This creates a location where concentrated pressure and flow of water can be used to turn turbines or water wheels. These can then drive an electric generator.

4.11.   The Kyoto Protocol

- Aim: reduce emission of greenhouse gases
- Countries agree to achieve stabilization of greenhouse gas concentrations in the atmosphere
- Countries agree to allow ecosystems to adapt naturally to climate change
- Developed countries should reduce their annual emissions by 5.2 per cent by 2008 (from the 1990 level)

4.12.   International peacekeeping at the turn of the century

4.12.1.   The United States

- Global policeman, only political superpower after the Cold war
- Economic pressure and military inventions (e.g. in Afghanistan)
- Showed their active global role in its own self-interest, but other countries expect help
- September 11th, 2001: terrorist attack on World Trade Centre → turning point "war on terrorism" ⇨ demonstrating power.

4.12.2.   The United Nations

- Group of 51 countries (October 24, 1945)
- Preserve international peace and security
- Promote friendly relations between member countries
- Support international cooperation with regard to economic, social and cultural and humanitarian issues

4.12.3.   International peacekeeping

- One of the aims of the UN
- Peacekeepers are sent to countries in question to oversee the peace process
- UN peacekeepers are soldiers (also police officers or civilian personnel; there is no UN military)
- Regional organizations (e.g. NATO) can be authorized by the UN
  - o to lead peacekeeping missions

- E.g.:
  - Kashmir
    - Kashmir Conflict (since 1949)

5. Shakespeare

5.1. William Shakespeare

- Born in Stratford approx. 23 April 1564 and died approx. in 23 April 1616
- Son of John and Mary Shakespeare
- 3rd children out of 8
- Received excellent education with heavy focus on grammar and literature
- Marriage to Anne Hathaway in November 1582 (he 18, she 26)
- Had three children ⇨ Susanna, Judith and Hamnet
- Became a person of interest in London in 1592

5.2. Elizabethan Age

5.2.1. Politics and economics

- Queen Elizabeth ruled for over 50 years (she died in 1603)
- England emerged as a world power
- International trade ⇨ rise of capitalism
- Strongest naval force
- Internal problems: constant clash between Catholics and Protestant ⇨ firm establishment of Protestant Church with Queen Elizabeth as the head of the Church of England

5.2.2. Culture

- Golden Age ⇨ term used for the Renaissance in Britain at the time of Elizabeth I
- Era was dominated by contrast: life for ordinary people could be hard, but economic growth also meant better conditions for many
- Negative aspects ⇨ harsh criminal laws, illiteracy, short life-expectancy, no rights for women
- Positive aspects ⇨ few beggars, public provision for the poor

5.3. The Great Chain of Being

- Vertical chain hierarchically ordered ⇨ universal order
- The more the spirit the higher the place in the chain

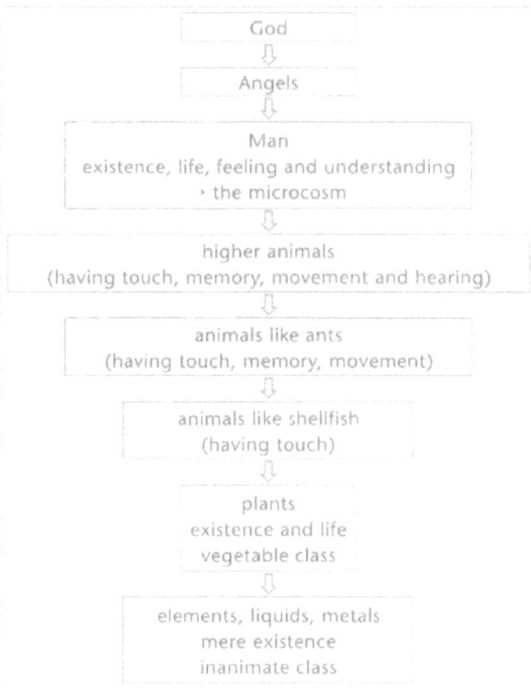

5.4. Elizabethan Theatre

5.4.1.Theatres

- Were situated outside the city
- Offered performance every day
- Presented plays, dances and music
- Were also used for bear baiting , cruel killing of bears
- All performances were presented during the day
- No lighting or special sound effects
- Women's roles were played by men
  ⇨ Imagination depended totally on the language used in the play

5.4.2.Common complaints about the theatre

- Disorderly
- Corrupts youth
- Leads to lewdness
- Attracts criminals
- Keep people away from work and prayer

5.5. Shakespeare's Language

Elizabethan English	Modern English
Thou	You (used for children, friends etc.)
Ye , you	You (plural
Thee	You(object form)

17

Art	Are
Mine	My
Doth, hath	Does, has
Thou canst, thou wilt	You can, you will
You know not	You can't know

5.6. Renaissance

- Immense cultural change
- Roots in Italy; 14th century to 17th century in England
- Many inventions ⇨ telescope, printing press etc. ⇨ people were provided with new insights
- Outbreaks of infectious diseases (plague)
- More people had access to books and learning ⇨ time of great learning and great art

5.7. Relevance to modern audience

Pros	Cons
Topics are still important ⇨ timeless/universal	Language is too difficult to understand
A lot of irony & economic elements; entertaining	Too old, not interesting
Image-filled and beautiful language, interesting	Topics are old-fashioned
A lot of new literature is based on the ideas of Shakespeare	Students who become workers or mechanics don't need to know anything about Shakespeare; not necessarily required
Reflects culture and history	Outdated attitude and values

6. Science and Ethics

6.1. Genetic engineering in general

6.1.1. Definition

- Deliberate, controlled manipulation of genes in an organism
- Isolating gene from one organism (donor)
- Putting isolated gene into another organism (recipient)
- Used to change appearance, intelligence, character etc.
- Nowadays focused on agriculture

6.1.2. Stem cells

- A cell in the body that is able to develop into any one of various kinds of cells
- Can divide without limit to replenish other cells and serve as a sort of repair system
- Pluripotent ⇨ able to make cells from all three basic body layers
- Omnipotent ⇨ can differentiate into embryonic and extraembryonic cell types
- Multipotent ⇨ ability to self-renew for long periods of time and differentiate into specialized cells with specific functions

6.1.3. Pros and Cons

Pros	Cons
Allows to interfile couples to have children	Stop In evolution
Be free of hereditary diseases	Tamper with nature
Donate organs, human tissue etc.	Make irrevocable mistakes

6.2. Genetically modified food (GM food)

6.2.1. General information

- Food that is genetically manipulated ⇨ to increase different factors like quicker growth etc.

6.2.2. Pros and Cons

Pros	Cons
Higher productivity	Genes can end up in unexpected places
(more) Resistant against weather and insects	Genes can mutate with harmful effect
More efficient land use	Transfer of allergic genes
Longer shelf life	GM products in the food chain
Growing crops in difficult growing conditions	Some Insects could become extinct
Rehabilitation of damaged land	Unknown consequences to the environment and health
More ecological farming	Large corporations would dominate agriculture

6.3. Cloning

6.3.1. General information

- Creation of an organism that is an exact genetic copy of another
- Raises moral and ethical concerns
- I.e. Dolly the sheep

6.3.2. Therapeutic Cloning

- Procedure for repairing/replacing damaged tissues and organs

6.3.3. Reproductive Cloning

- Procedure with the goal of planting the blastula (=early developmental stage of an organism) produced by the technique into the uterus (=Gebärmutter) of an adult female and thus creating new organisms.

6.3.4. DNA-Cloning

- Procedure to produce multiple copies of a single gene or segment of DNA

6.4. Designer baby

6.4.1. General information

- Baby whose genetic makeup has been artificially selected to ensure the presence or absence of certain characteristics, especially with regard to the sex of the child

6.4.2. Pros and Cons

Pros	Cons
Often last chance for a couple to get a healthy child	Not 100% save that your child is completely healthy and without any diseases
A "save" healthy child	Very expensive
You can "create" your own child (⇨modify)	Difficult decision for the parents ⇨ critical seen in the society

6.5. Glossary

6.5.1. Reprogenetics

Pros	Cons
Parents have a right to choose	Technology is not safe yet
Moral obligation to give children the best life possible	Bioethical codes condemn experiments with human beings
Will lead to improvement of the whole species	"imperfect" human beings would be discriminated against

6.5.2. Sex selection

Pros	Cons
Parents have a right to choose	Preferences patriarchal cultures lead to demographic imbalance
In some cultures male offspring are important to provide support for old age	Members of the unwanted sex may be discriminated against

6.5.3. Human cloning

Pros	Cons
Medical Reason: resource of bone marrow or replaceable organs	Cloning is inherently evil, an intrusion into human life
Infertile couples may have children	Children may be thought of as products

6.5.4. In vitro fertilization

- Male and female cells are brought together in a test tube to create a human embryo

YOUR KNOWLEDGE HAS VALUE